# The Holy Spirit:
## The Feminine Nature of God

*How the feminine component of
Jehovah God was erased from
early Christian and Jewish beliefs*

## Patricia Taylor

iUniverse, Inc.
New York Bloomington

**The Holy Spirit: The Feminine Nature of God**
How the feminine component of Jehovah God was
erased from early Christian and Jewish beliefs

iUniverse books may be ordered through booksellers or by contacting:

iUniverse
1663 Liberty Drive
Bloomington, IN 47403
www.iuniverse.com
1-800-Authors (1-800-288-4677)

ISBN: 978-1-4401-7484-1 (pbk)
ISBN: 978-1-4401-7485-8 (ebk)

Printed in the United States of America

iUniverse rev. date: 9/24/2009

Worship is giving God the best that He has given you. Be careful what you do with the best you have. Whenever you get a blessing from God, give it back to Him as a love gift. Take time to meditate before God and offer the blessing back to Him in a deliberate act of worship. If you hoard a thing of blessing for your self, it will turn into spiritual dry rot, as the manna did when it was hoarded. God will never let you hold a spiritual thing for your self, it has to be given back to Him that He may make it a blessing to others.

It is impossible to keep our moral practices sound and our inward attitudes right while our idea of God is erroneous or inadequate. If we would bring back spiritual power to our lives, we must begin to think of God more nearly as He is.

**...If you hold to my teaching, you are really my disciples. Then you will know the truth and the truth will set you free. (John 8:31-32)**

I offer this book as a "love gift" to our God,
and I pray He uses it to bless others.

# *Acknowledgements*

I wish to thank my husband, Jerry, who has supported and encouraged this effort for many years. He has provided an environment that frees me to read, write and meditate on the word of God.

# *Contents*

# Introduction

This is a book about the nature of God. Since mankind was created in the image of God, we can know ourselves better by understanding the true nature of God. God is the God of truth and we must worship Him in spirit and in truth. The God of Abraham, Isaac, Ishmael and Jacob is a triune God; God the Father, God the Son and God the Holy Spirit.

The Holy Spirit is clearly feminine in nature and is the part of God reflected in womanhood. I have relied on Scripture, the Apocrypha and other early, credible Christian writings to reveal this quality of the Holy Spirit.

The writings of several Apostolic Fathers supported this understanding, but as time went by, mainstream Christianity considered any reference to a feminine divinity heresy. Throughout history, many Christian mystics continued to think of God in both feminine and masculine terms. They included Julian of Norwich, Mechthild of Hackeborn, Christina of Markgate, St. Birgitta of Sweden, Anselm of Canterbury, Meister Eckhart and Bernard of Clairvoux (1, Oxford-Carpenter). St. Hildegard of Bingen lived in the 12th century and was not only accomplished in writing, composing and church leadership, but she also became an advisor to bishops, popes and kings. She believed it is God's maternal love that opens us to repentance.

Albert Einstein once said that Israel would not experience salvation until it returned to feminine divinity. Carl Jung felt true equality between men and women would be tied to the acceptance of a concrete, personal "divine woman." Several modern day writers have addressed the feminine aspect of God and the nurturing, mothering qualities found throughout Scripture. Most of them ignore the person of the Trinity who would reflect this aspect of the nature of God, while a few attribute this aspect to the Holy Spirit.

I am not a theologian, pastor, evangelist or formally trained in any way. I am not even an author. I have never seriously considered taking on the daunting task of writing a book. As far as credentials go, I am a nobody. This is an aspect of God's nature that is so refreshing. He loves to use nobodies to carry out His plan for mankind. When He told Gideon He would use him to save the Israelite people from the oppression of the Midianites, Gideon said his family was the weakest of his tribe and that he was the weakest of his family. David and Joseph were both the youngest and weakest, in a worldly sense, in their families. And, of course, Jesus came as a carpenter's son from a small, insignificant town. He chose uneducated fishermen and other unimportant people in society to carry His message to the world. Paul said, "…**I am a nobody" (NAS, 2Corinthians 12:11).**

Writing this book in no way compares to what was done by these men, but it is an example of how God works through people who are completely powerless and unknown. He reaches down and says, "I will use *you* to accomplish this thing. That way everyone will know it is I, God of heaven and earth, who has done it."

I have read extensively and have had the freedom to listen to many great speakers on Christian radio. My only credential is that I am a Spirit-filled Christian. I believe God is alive, and not only working in the lives of His children, but also using those who are available to accomplish His work in today's world. I continue to seek to understand more of how God works in this world and what my part is in revealing His kingdom to my brothers and sisters.

I feel a need to give a brief background of my spiritual path. Do not think I have always been a strong Christian, or that I grew up in a Christian home where I received a solid foundation of Christian teaching. My parents never went to church, and I do not remember there being a Bible in our home until I was in high school. They were good, hardworking people who did their best to provide their children with a fairly normal family life. They were both raised in the church, and I think they both believed in God and accepted Christ as the Son of God; but as adults, they did not appear to be seeking God or His ways.

When I was in high school, I went to a Christian movie and afterward heard a taped message by Billy Graham. I accepted Christ as the Son of God and as my savior. I believe I experienced conversion by the Holy Spirit and received the gift of faith, but I did not accept Jesus as Lord of my life. I then went back to the same non-Christian environment. I did not know how to *be* a Christian, and there was no one in my immediate surroundings to show me how to start on the path of Christian living. I received no discipleship.

It saddens me to think of what I missed out on because I was ignorant of the life available to me in Christ. I did not seek Christ or His ways. I walked on my own, doing the best I could, not following Him or His word. I lived a life very similar to those around me. I lived in sin because I was not following God. Because I did not claim what He promised, I feel like He let me wander in the wilderness forty years, just as the Israelites did. The year I turned forty, He reached down and grabbed me out of the chaos of my life and shook me. That started a process that led me to accepting Him as Lord of my life.

God has used my pastors and many authors and speakers to bring me to this understanding of who He is. I am not saying I know all there is to know about God. I am still on my journey and I will not see Him clearly until I meet Him face to face. However, God wants us to seek Him and He reveals more and more of Himself to those who do.

His greatest tool in revealing Himself to me is the Holy Spirit. Without the Holy Spirit working in my heart, I could not understand the things of God, and I would never have come to the understanding of the Holy Spirit being the feminine nature of God. There is no gender in heaven, but each person of the trinity clearly has a different nature and function. By understanding this difference and by accepting that the earthly family is a reflection of this godly relationship, we can better understand the nature of men and women and apply this understanding to our human family and relationships.

Man was created for relationships, and if our relationships are not healthy and fulfilling, life has no real value. Through a clearer understanding of our intrinsic nature, we can better interpret the world around us and find that place of comfort and fulfillment we all desire.

As I came to this understanding of the feminine nature of the Holy Spirit, it seemed so obvious. Scripture and other historical writings support this truth. Has God chosen this particular time to bring back the knowledge of this aspect of His nature to His followers, or have believers deliberately chosen not to put forward a truth that is contradictory to traditional translations? I do not know why He revealed this to me or lead me to write about it, but I do know I have to obey His leading and His purpose for my life. I want the abundant life He promises, and it is not available to me if I am not willing to obey Him.

Most Christians today rely only on the Bible and current Christian writers and teachers for their understanding of God and as their reference for Christian living. The Bible truly is an amazing and even supernatural book. I believe it is the inspired word of God given to us so we can know Him and learn to live a life pleasing to Him. As Hebrews 4:12 says, the word of God is living and active. If you long to find God, He can be found through study and reflection on His word. If you have a problem, the solution is there if you search for it.

The Bible is a book that is just as pertinent for us today as it was when it was first compiled. It was written for all times and for all people. If you study the words of Jesus, you will find He seldom addressed current issues of the time. His teachings were eternal. They addressed who we are, how we are to treat each other, and how we can have an intimate relationship with God. Man has not changed. We have the same needs and weaknesses man had two thousand years ago. We have the same longings for peace and purpose. Jesus addressed not only our basic human nature, but also our spiritual nature. What He had to say is as important for us today as it was for the people of biblical times.

I believe the Bible is the word of God and that the Spirit of God inspired the original writers, but I also believe there have been some mistranslations over time. I believe parts of the Bible were written addressing specific situations and problems of a particular time. God meets us where we are, and this needs to be taken into consideration when studying scripture.

There are many other writings that are valuable for information and clarification of the things of God. The Apocrypha is a group of books written between about 300 BC and the birth of Christ. Most of them were originally written in Greek and were included in the original Septuagint or Greek translation of the Old Testament. They were considered canon by the early church and also included in the first Latin Bible, the Vulgate, edited by Jerome in 400 AD (2, Harrop). The Vulgate became the authorized Bible of Western Europe and England for the next 1000 years. The Puritans of the 1600s were the first to request Bibles without these books. Within the last 200 years, they have been eliminated from Protestant Bibles. They are still found in the Catholic Bible and are also valued and used by Orthodox Christians (3, Goodspeed).

There are other writings by the Apostolic Fathers, the early church leaders, that are very important for understanding church history and the origins of our Christian traditions. I believe they can be used to better understand Judeo and Christian beliefs that have been lost or eliminated for different reasons. There are also many writings that have been determined to be part or all myth.

Some of these writings may have been inspired by God or possibly none of them were. I have not approached them as inspired, but I do believe they can be used to verify and clarify ideas and beliefs found in scripture. They definitely reflect the beliefs of early Christians.

In late 1996, I sent a letter to four radio evangelists that I respected and listened to regularly asking if the Holy Spirit could be feminine. I found the response from their ministries quite interesting. One did not respond at all, one sent a form letter not addressing my question and the third criticized me for concluding that the qualities of God and the relationship within the Godhead can be used to define the relationship between husbands and wives. One of the four agreed that God "contains male and female concepts" and admitted the possibility that the Holy Spirit could be the feminine nature of God.

What is so interesting to me is that this corresponds to the parable of the sower. Only one in four who hears the word of God understands it and continues in it to produce a godly life. The truth is important to God, and through the Spirit of Truth, or the Holy Spirit, He will reveal it.

I have used many sources to substantiate this truth, but I am sure there is much more evidence that can be considered. One of the goals of this book is to initiate a dialogue among Christian leaders and theologians addressing this aspect of God. Jewish theologians should be included since much of the evidence originates in the Old Testament.

This book is not just for Christians and those who follow Jehovah God. It is based on the Bible and other Christian writings, but it reflects truths that are inherent to mankind. The Bible reveals these truths, but they are also recognized by the study of human nature. The understanding of our God being both male and female is life changing and will affect society around us. Every person should have an interest in the truths put forth in this writing.

I believe promoting the masculinity of God and eliminating His feminine nature has done not only women, but also mankind in general, a great disservice. It has negated the important position of women in the home, church and society. The result was the women's liberation movement which strived to make women the same as men and to give women the same position as men. I believe women have a wonderful, God-given position that is equal to but different from men. I pray one of the things this book accomplishes is giving all women a sense of self-worth and value that Jesus promoted while He was on this earth.

I write this at a time when our world is torn by religious conflict and violence, not only between Christians and Muslims and differing sects of Islam, but also between the religious and non-religious. There is so much hate that spurs this on. The only way these factions can live in peace is by allowing love to influence and soften differences. For this to happen, women have to step into their god-given roles that can influence every situation. I believe the nature of the woman, being the weaker vessel (physically), but the stronger relational love-giver, is the catalyst that can resolve the violence in our families and the world. This is especially pertinent in the Muslim world where the influence of women has been repressed. They need to teach their children about love and peace and the devastating results of hatred and revenge.

I have come to an understanding about my *privileges* and *responsibilities* as a child of God. There are many things I have no control over and I must give them up to God. My part in our relationship is to serve Him wholeheartedly, working for His Kingdom on this earth. When I do this, God is concerned about what concerns me. My greatest concerns deal with my loved ones coming to accept God's truth. Only God can prepare a heart to hear and receive that truth.

A greater goal of this book is to inspire others to seek God and His true nature. The entire Bible was written and compiled to help us know Jehovah God, the God of Abraham, Isaac and Jacob. It is only through knowing and loving God that we find peace and fulfillment in this life. The more accurate our understanding of who He is, the more mature and productive our relationships with Him can be.

I have taken over ten years to finish this small book. I have let many things get in the way, but I feel I have to finish it to get on with my life. I must put it out there and let God use it as He pleases. I trust God has brought me to this place in His time and that the time is perfect. I pray this book is a blessing to those who love God and an inspiration for those who do not to get to know Him better.

# Notes

1. Rebecca Oxford-Carpenter, "Gender and the Trinity," *Theology Today*, Vol. 41, No. 1, April, 1984.
2. Clayton Harrop, *Holman Bible Dictionary*, (Nashville: Holman Bible Publishers, 1991,) p. 69.
3. Edgar J. Goodspeed, *The Apocrypha*, (New York, NY: Vintage Books, A Division of Random House, Inc., 1989,) p. v.

# Chapter 1

## *In the Beginning*

**In the beginning God created the heavens and the earth. Now the earth was formless and empty, darkness was over the surface of the deep, and the Spirit of God was hovering over the waters. (Genesis 1:1-2)**

**In the beginning was the Word, and the Word was with God, and the Word was God. He was with God in the beginning. (John 1:1-2)**

It is important to know and understand the one true God. He created the heavens and the earth and all that inhabit them. Knowing Him and how He created us helps us understand ourselves better and leads to a healthier, productive life.

**...the LORD is God in heaven above and on the earth below. There is no other. (Deuteronomy 4:39)**

1

> **…Before me no god was formed, nor will there be one after me. (Isaiah 43:10)**
>
> **Now this is eternal life: that they may know you, the only true God… (John 17:3)**
>
> **Now to the King eternal, immortal, invisible, the only God, be honor and glory for ever and ever. Amen. (1Timothy 1:17)**

People often refer to the god of the Muslims, the god of the Jews, the god of Buddha, the New Age god, etc., as if they have a different god than Christians do; but there is only one true God. He reveals Himself to mankind through His Word, nature and the Holy Spirit. Jesus came to die for our redemption, but in the process, He also revealed more of who the Father is. He said if you have seen Me, you have seen the Father. After His death and resurrection, the Holy Spirit was sent to indwell the children of God and empower them to continue the work of Jesus on earth, making disciples of God and growing the family of God (the Church).

> **"I the LORD do not change…" (Malachi 3:6)**
>
> **…the Father of heavenly lights, who does not change like shifting shadows. (James 1:17)**

All mankind was created with a spirit, and that spirit has a need to worship. Anthropologists have noted that worship is a part of our human nature. We are programmed with every fiber of our being to seek a connection with God. If we fail to worship God, we always find a substitute, whether it is a false god, another person, material things, or even ourselves (1, Warren).

Down through the ages, man has come up with many interpretations of the unseen world of God and ways to interact with it. Different cultures have developed different gods to worship. They are all perversions of different aspects of the one true God. They include not only male gods, but also many female goddesses. They are the result of mankind trying to interpret the spiritual kingdom around them through their limited, human senses.

As we read history and look around the world today, we see examples of the misguided results of this effort. The Hebrews, or Jews, were not exempt from this. Although God revealed Himself to them through many prophets and miracles, they consistently ended up worshiping false gods.

But where have those gods gone? Does anyone still believe in Baal, Zeus, Aphrodite, Demeter, Isis or the hundreds of other gods worshipped down through history? Was there any *truth* in these beliefs if they have all faded? The knowledge of Jehovah, God of Abraham, Isaac and Jacob, has survived at least 5,000 years. He has revealed more and more of Himself to man over time, but He is the same God Adam and Eve fellowshipped with in the Garden, and He has not changed.

Many today like to believe they have an accurate understanding of who God is. It is very likely we have not only misinterpreted some of His revelation, but also man has bent or shaped revelation to fit his desire of who he thinks God should be. I believe the misconception of the nature of the Holy Spirit is an example of this.

Abraham, the first Hebrew, is considered the father of Judaism, Christianity, and Islam because of the covenant God made with him. This covenant represents God's plan of redemption for mankind. Why God chose Abraham to initiate this plan and to bring a more accurate revelation of who He is to mankind, we cannot know. The time was probably right, the place was right. Abraham must have had a heart open to God and His plan. I have wondered if another reason could have been Abraham's ability or desire to record history. Whether originally oral or written, it resulted in a written history of God's dealings with Abraham and His promise to him and his descendants. These writings of the Hebrews resulted in the Old Testament, which has been preserved for thousands of years.

The Old Testament records times when God would send the Holy Spirit to give special knowledge and ability to individuals to accomplish His purposes. I believe the first alphabet based language is an example of this. "Alphabets apparently arose only once in human history: among speakers of Semitic languages (Jews), in the area from modern Syria to the Sinai (Canaan), during the second millennium BC (Abraham's time). All of the hundreds of historical and now existing alphabets were ultimately derived from that one ancestral Semitic alphabet…" (2, Diamond, parentheses added).

The Old Testament is a history of the Israelite people, but more than that, it is a history of God's dealings with man. I believe God wants us to know Him, and the Old Testament is a record of God revealing Himself and establishing a covenant relationship with mankind. Through this process, He revealed His nature.

In the Hebrew culture, a name was a reflection of the nature of the individual. The Hebrews gave God many names reflecting His nature revealed to them through His interaction with them. Yahweh (YHWH) or Jehovah, I am or covenant; Adonis, lord or master; Yahweh-jireh, the God who provides; Yahweh-rophe, the God who heals; Yahweh-shalom, God of my peace; etc. El Shaddai, Almighty God, emphasized God's nurturing, relational qualities that are seen in the nature of the Holy Spirit. This name for God is used at least seven times in scripture, and in both Hebrew and Aramaic, it means full-breasted.

**Then God said, "Let us make man in our *image*, in our *likeness*, and let them rule**

> **over the fish of the sea and the birds of the air, over the livestock, over all the earth, and over all the creatures that move along the ground." So God created man in his own image, in the image of God he created him; male and female he created them. (Genesis 1:26-27, italics added)**

God is a triune God. The three persons of God—God the Father, God the Holy Spirit, and God the Son (or Word)—are eternal and existed before the creation of the world. Together, they created the heavens and the earth. The name used for God in the creation is Elohim, which signifies plurality.

> **The LORD God said, "It is not good for the man to be alone. I will make a helper suitable for him." (Genesis 2:18)**

> **So the LORD God caused the man to fall into a deep sleep; and while he was sleeping, he took one of the man's ribs (NIV Disciples Study Bible footnotes say, "a portion of man's side") and closed up the place with flesh. Then the LORD God made a woman from the rib he had taken out of the man, and he brought her to the man. (Genesis 2:21-22, parenthesis added)**

When "man" is used in scripture, it often refers to mankind. Mankind includes male and female. It takes male and female to express the *image* and *likeness* of God. God created man, Adam, in His own image and said it is not good for man to be alone. He caused the man to sleep and He separated him into two beings. He took the feminine nature or characteristics from Adam and created Eve. Adam expresses this separation of his body by describing woman as **"bone of my bone and flesh of my flesh" (Genesis 2:23).**

When Scripture says man was created in God's *image*, it refers to the spirit of man. God created man of the dust of the earth and breathed His Spirit into him. Man is both a physical and a spiritual being. By understanding this, we can better realize our dual nature. We have a physical nature and a spiritual nature. We have both physical and spiritual needs that strive to be met. If we fail to recognize our spiritual needs and only meet the physical needs of our flesh, the spirit suffers.

The spirit cannot be seen, but it is more important than the physical. We can go for a time satisfying the physical and get away with it, but the time will come when God will not be ignored. He will bring us to a place of despair and it is only by turning to Him and healing our spirits that we find a place of balance, health and order in our lives. If we do not embrace our spiritual natures and meet our spiritual needs, we live in darkness.

> The singular "man" is created as a plurality, "male and female." In a similar way the one God ("and God said") created humankind through an expression of his plurality ("Let us make man in our image"). Following this clue the divine plurality expressed in v. 26 is seen as an anticipation of the human plurality of the man and woman, thus casting the human relationship between man and woman as a reflection of God's own personal relationship with himself." (3, Sailhamer)

**Hear, O Israel: The LORD our God, the LORD is one.
(Deuteronomy 6:4)**

Jon Courson in his teaching of Deuteronomy and the Shama explains the Hebrew word, "echod," is used to describe the oneness of a triune God. It signifies a "compound unity." It is also used to describe the "one curtain" of the Tabernacle, which was actually many curtains that created "one" curtain. Genesis 2:24 says a man and a woman are to be united and become one (echod) flesh, two entities that work, or function, as one. This union is a symbol or type that reflects the "oneness" of God; three natures that function as one.

The family of God includes Jesus, the begotten son, not created out of nothing as the rest of creation, but of the same substance as God. God ordained mankind to raise godly children and it is a natural urge for mankind to unite and produce an earthly family that reflects the heavenly family. Begotten children, produced by the mother and father and of the same substance.

> ...man's creation "in God's image" also entails a "partnership" (NIV "a suitable helper (GK 6469)") with his wife. The "likeness" that the man and the woman share with God in chapter 1 finds an analogy in the "likeness" between the man and his wife in chapter 2. (4, Sailhamer)

The likeness of God included in man is his function or role. By creating mankind in His own likeness, God intended the relationship between man and woman, and within our families, to reflect the relationship within the triune Godhead. He intended the earthly family to reflect the family of God, and it is in our marriage relationship that we most clearly reflect the image and likeness of the trinity. As humans, we can never attain the perfection of this godly relationship; but if we embrace this truth and rely on the perfect example, we may greatly enhance the quality of our earthly relationships and family life.

A friend once asked me why I thought God created man (Adam) as one being and then separated him into two (Adam and Eve), when He had created the animals male and female originally. I had to think about it for a while, but it occurred to me that it is another example of man being created in the image of God. "In the beginning" refers to God's creation of heaven and earth, but that was not the beginning of God. God was one, but before He created the heavens and earth, He somehow *split His nature or essence* which resulted in the Holy Spirit (Paraclete or helper) and Jesus (the Word), the only begotten son. (Explained further in Chapter 2)

As I have focused my study on this aspect of God, it has occurred to me that this is the key to all of creation and man's purpose on earth. Yes, God instructed us to populate and care for the earth, but in doing this, we are to glorify Him. How do we do this more perfectly than by reflecting His image into this physical world? Jesus glorified God by speaking His words and by doing what the Father sent Him to do. We glorify God by reflecting Him, the trinity, through our family relationships.

### Notes

1.  Rick Warren, *The Purpose Driven Life*, (Grand Rapids, Michigan: Zondervan, 2002) p. 64.
2.  Jared Diamond, *Guns, Germs, and Steel*, (New York, NY: W.W. Norton and Company, 1999) p. 226.
3.  John H. Sailhamer, *Zondervan NIV Bible Commentary*, Genesis, (Grand Rapids, Michigan: Zondervan, 1994) p. 6.
4.  Sailhamer, p. 8

# Chapter 2

## *The Paraclete*

God is one, but there are three persons or natures of God; God the Father, God the Holy Spirit and God the Son. This is hard for us in our human minds to comprehend, but we find the truth of this throughout scripture. Each person of the trinity has a distinctive nature and role, though this is sometimes blurred by the names used in the Old Testament and the emphasis given through human reporting. It is clear that each has a distinct and prominent place in the work of God.

In the Old Testament, the work of God the Father was especially emphasized. Jehovah God was the author of the physical world. With the Holy Spirit at His side and the Word (Jesus Christ), they created the world and mankind. When His plan was marred by Adam and Eve in the garden, He set in motion His plan of redeeming mankind through the Messiah, Jesus Christ. His covenant with Abraham was the initiation of this process. He chose the Israelites to be a unique people who would take His truth to all nations. It was a relationship of master and servant. He blessed and prospered the Israelites when they followed and obeyed Him, and disciplined them when they did not.

During the life of Jesus, the redeeming work of the Son was prominent. He came to convince the Jews that He was their Messiah prophesied in the Old Testament. When they denied Him, He gave up His life as an atoning sacrifice so all mankind could be reconciled to God. He also established the New Covenant of grace and unconditional love. Those who received Him became the children of God.

Since Pentecost, the saving and empowering work of the Holy Spirit has been the primary factor in God's kingdom work. Her loving, nurturing, counseling qualities facilitate the relationships required to build the body of Christ and to develop mature Christians.

The Holy Spirit is the "mysterious" third person of the Trinity, considered mysterious probably because Scripture does not expound on Her nature as much as the Father and the Son. The union of the Holy Spirit and the spirit of a person, how that happens and what the manifested results are, is a mysterious thing. In scripture, distinguishing between the actions of the Father, the Son and the Holy Spirit is not easy because the name God, or Lord, is used in different places to refer to each one.

The Spirit of God was active in the Old Testament, beginning with creation, in nature and among God's people, guiding and delivering them. She manifested Herself as an impersonal force to do great physical things, such as the parting of the Red Sea, and providing guidance and sustenance for the Israelites as they traveled through the dessert and went into the Promised Land. The Holy Spirit also indwelled individuals such as King David, the prophets and the judges to give great insight or extraordinary strength. After Jesus ascended to heaven, God sent the Holy Spirit to indwell believers to empower them to accomplish the work of God. As our teacher and counselor, She also reveals to us the things of God. The Holy Spirit is not just a force. She clearly is a person of the Trinity with intellect, emotions and will.

We have seen that the Holy Spirit is a person, and is God, and is a member of the Trinity. Anyone who fails to recognize this is robbed of his joy and power. Of course a defective view of any member of the Trinity will bring about this result because God is all important. But this is especially true for the Holy Spirit, for although the Father is the source of all blessing, and the Son is the channel of all blessing, it is through the Holy Spirit at work in us that all truth becomes living and operative in our lives. (1, Graham)

Jesus told his followers, **"If you love me, you will obey what I command. And I will ask the Father, and he will give you another Counselor to be with you forever—the Spirit of truth" (John 14:15-17). "…Unless I go away, the Counselor (Paraclete) will not come to you; but if I go, I will send him to you" (John 16:7, parentheses added).** I find it very interesting that the New American Standard Bible has chosen to translate the word "Paraclete" as "Helper" instead of "Counselor"; a clear reminder of Eve's role as a helper.

In Genesis, the description of Eve as a companion for Adam closely reflects this quality of the Holy Spirit as helper (counselor), comforter and *one called alongside.*

The expression describing this companion (Eve) literally means "a helper corresponding to him" or *"a helper alongside of him,"* a beautiful description of the relationship which God intends between husband and wife. (2, NIV Disciples Study Bible, italics and brackets added)

Paraclete, the Greek word used for Holy Spirit, literally means *one called alongside*, and is translated advocate, comforter, and counselor (3, Butler). In the original Hebrew of the Old Testament and in Aramaic of the New Testament, the gender of the Holy Spirit is feminine. The Septuagint was the first translation of the Old Testament from Hebrew to Greek. Great care was taken to do this accurately. Despite this effort, the gender of the feminine Hebrew word, "ruach," was changed to the Greek word, "pneuma," which is neuter. When Jerome translated the Greek into the Latin Vulgate, the gender of "spirit" was changed from neuter to masculine.

Yes, the pronoun "he" is accepted if the gender is unknown, but it is clear the gender of spirit was originally feminine. The pronoun "She" should be used if an accurate translation is desired. This is historical fact that cannot be denied, but it is overlooked by Bible teachers today. It is an example of the influence man has had on scripture since its original writing. These slight changes over time have resulted in a patriarchal church and society that have prevented women from bringing a healthy influence and balance to the church. It has also given them a second class status in society and the family that has been difficult to overcome.

Early Christians understood and accepted this family relationship and equality within the Godhead. In the first 200 years after Christ, women enjoyed ecclesiastical power in the church and androgynous images of God were common. Gnosticism was a sect of early Christianity that accepted the equality of men and women in God's Kingdom, but it also promoted a secret knowledge that was accessible to only a few. This group was considered heretical by church leaders and eventually stamped out. Cultural and political trends lead to an increasingly patriarchal church and God's image was masculinized (4, Oxford-Carpenter).

This elimination of the feminine aspect of God also occurred in the Hebrew or Jewish teachings. God's presence with man on earth was given the name Shekhinah. This was the name used to describe the part of God that dwells in the world and was feminine. She guided the Israelites through the desert and rested on the tabernacle and early temple. She was also considered to be the Bride of God. "...despite the feminine gender of the Hebrew word 'Shekhinah,' the Rabbis went to great efforts to emphasize that the Shekhinah is no one else but the familiar (male) God of the Hebrew Bible" (5, Schafer).

There may be several reasons the early religious leaders, both Christian and Jewish, went to such great lengths to cleanse their writings of a feminine nature of God. One was probably the concern that the one true God would be adulterated into individual pagan gods. Throughout scripture, the Israelites were drawn into worshipping female pagan gods as well as male. This even occurred in Temple worship (2Kings 21). If two or three gods had been worshipped instead of one with a triune nature, there was the concern of the first monotheistic religion turning into a polytheistic religion.

Another explanation I see for this was man's desire not to give a feminine nature such a prominent place in their lives. Until Christ, women were very insignificant in the family and in society. It was even debated as to whether women had souls. If the Holy Spirit indwelled believers, men would not want to embrace the Holy Spirit's feminine nature. The Holy Spirit, as one person of the Trinity, is equal to the Father and the Son. Accepting the Holy Spirit as feminine in nature, gives women an equal position with men and equal importance in God's plan for mankind. This would obviously have been a deterrent to spreading Christianity in the early years.

Jews and Muslims accept Jesus as a great prophet but not as the Son of God, and they do not recognize the giving of the Holy Spirit reported at Pentecost; but the Holy Spirit is very evident in the Old Testament, and God promised He would pour out His Spirit on all people (Joel 2:28).

The Bible refers to the Holy Spirit, or the Spirit of God, as the Spirit of Truth (John 14:17, 16:13, 1John 4:6), and also as the Spirit of Wisdom (Isaiah 11:2, Deuteronomy 34:9, Ephesians 1:17). Joshua, Moses' successor, was filled with the Spirit of God (Numbers 27:18), but in the same context in Deuteronomy 34:9, this spirit is called the "spirit of wisdom." Another situation where the Spirit of God is equated with the Spirit of Wisdom is the craftsmen who were indwelled by God to enable them to build the tabernacle. Exodus 31:3 and 35:31 explain how the skilled craftsmen and women were filled by the Spirit of God. In Exodus 28:3, God refers to the craftsmen He **"endowed with the spirit of wisdom"** (NAS). God puts His Spirit in our hearts (2Corinthians 1:22), and Wisdom will also enter our hearts (2Chronicles 9:23, Job 38:36, Proverbs 2:10, 14:33). It was these references that made me look more closely at the personification of Wisdom in Proverbs, and started my search for the connection between Wisdom and the Holy Spirit.

Wisdom is often said to be an "attribute" of God, but a feminine pronoun is always used to refer to Her. She is clearly a separate entity from God, the Father, just as Christ is separate from Him. Wisdom says, **"The LORD *brought me forth* as the first of his works, before his deeds of old; I was appointed from eternity, from the beginning, before the world began. When there were no oceans, I was *given birth*, when there were no springs abounding with water; before the mountains were settled in place, before the hills, I was given birth,"** (Proverbs 8:22-25 italics added). "I was there when he set the heavens in place..." (Proverbs 8:27). "Then I was the *craftsman at his side*..." (Proverbs 8:30, italics added).** This is another description of a helper alongside (Paraclete). The Holy Spirit and the Word (Jesus Christ) were active in the creation of the heavens and the earth. No one disputes this, but Wisdom was there also. **"By Wisdom the LORD laid the earth's foundations... (Proverbs 3:19).**

Somehow, the person of Wisdom has been separated from the Holy Spirit, but She is clearly the Holy Spirit.

# Other Comparisons in Scripture

There is much more evidence of this in scripture. Wisdom refers to those whom she is talking to as her sons (Proverbs 8), just as believers are called sons of God. Her instructions to her children are the same as God's to His children. The Book of Proverbs expresses over and over the benefits of the teachings, or counsel, of Wisdom. If we embrace them and live by them, we will find a long, healthy life that is peaceful, prosperous and successful. These are the same results promised to those who love the LORD and follow His precepts.

---

Scripture says referring to God's word:

> **"Your word is a lamp to my feet and a light for my path." (Psalm 119:105)**
> **"These commandments that I give you today are to be upon your hearts." (Deuteronomy 6:6)**
> **"…obey carefully all the words of this law. They are not just idle words for you—they are your life. By them you will live long in the land…" (Deuteronomy 32:46-47)**

Wisdom (the Holy Spirit) says:

> **"Blessed is the man who listens to me… For whoever finds me finds life and receives favor from the LORD." (Proverbs 8:34-35)**
> **"Now then, my sons, listen to me; blessed are those who keep my ways." (Proverbs 8:32)**
> **"…whoever listens to me will live in safety…" (Proverbs 1:33)**

Paul said God:

> **"...put his Spirit in our hearts..." (2Corinthians 1:22)**

Proverbs says:

> **"For the Lord gives wisdom..." (Proverbs 2:6)**
>
> **"...For wisdom will enter your heart..." (Proverbs 2:10)**

---

God says:

> **"...I will pour out my Spirit on your offspring..." (Isaiah 44:3)**
>
> **"Even on my servants, both men and women, I will pour out my Spirit..." (Joel 2:29)**

Wisdom (the Holy Spirit) says:

> **If you will respond to my rebuke, "...I will pour out my spirit on you..." (Proverbs 1:23, NAS)**

---

God says:

> **"Walk in all the way that the Lord your God has commanded you, so that you may live and prosper and prolong your days in the land that you will posses." (Deuteronomy 5:33)**

Wisdom (the Holy Spirit) says:

> **"For through me your days will be many, and years will be added to your life." (Proverbs 9:11)**

Jesus says:

>"Whoever has my commands and obeys them, he is the one who loves me. He who loves me will be loved by my Father, and I too will love him and show myself to him." (John 14:21)

Wisdom (the Holy Spirit) says:

>"I love those who love me…" (Proverbs 8:17)

---

Scripture says:

>If you seek God, you will find Him. (1Chronicles 28:9, 2Chronicles 15:2, Jeremiah 29:13, Matthew 7:8)

Wisdom (the Holy Spirit) says:

>"…those who seek me find me." (Proverbs 8:17)

---

Jesus says:

>"…I chose you and appointed you to go and bear fruit—fruit that will last…" (John 15:16)

Wisdom (the Holy Spirit) says:

>"My fruit is better than fine gold…" (Proverbs 8:19)

---

# Comparisons from the Book of Wisdom

The Book of Wisdom, or the Wisdom of Solomon, is part of the Apocrypha and is still considered Holy Scripture by Roman Catholics and greatly valued by Orthodox Christians. As mentioned earlier, the Apocrypha was eliminated from Protestant Bibles after the Reformation. These writings are unknown to most Protestants. The Book of Wisdom was written the first century BC (6, The New American Bible) and clearly equates Wisdom with the Holy Spirit.

It describes Wisdom as the Holy Spirit of instruction, sent by God from "on high" (Wisdom 9:17), who was present when God created the world (Wisdom 9:9). God guides Her (Wisdom 7:15), and She is the breath of the power of God (Wisdom 7:25, Goodspeed). The Bible also speaks of the Holy Spirit as the breath of God (Job 33:4, Psalm 33:6, Isaiah 30:33, John 20:22). Wisdom is described as a "starry flame by night" who guided the Israelites out of Egypt (Wisdom 10:17) and through the Red Sea (Wisdom 10:18). This coincides with Exodus 13:21: **"By day the Lord went ahead of them (the fleeing Israelites) in a pillar of cloud to guide them on their way and by night in a pillar of fire…"**

God loves Wisdom because She instructs about understanding God (Wisdom 8:4), and He sends Her to teach men what is pleasing to Him (Wisdom 9:9-10). She shares the all-knowing and all-powerful nature of God (Wisdom 7:23, 8:8). She is the *craftsman* who produces all things (Wisdom 8:5-6), who has fashioned and permeates all things (Wisdom 7:22, 24). She sits by God's throne (Wisdom 9:4) at His side, and is only dispatched from the Lord at His choosing (Wisdom 9:10). She counsels during good times and comforts during times of grief (Wisdom 8:9). "…and passing into holy souls, from age to age, she produces friends of God, and prophets" (Wisdom 7:27).

Just as the Bible says Moses was filled and guided by the Spirit of God (Numbers 11:17, 25, Joshua 3:7, Isaiah 63:12), Wisdom 10:16 says, "She (Wisdom) entered the soul of the Lord's servant (Moses)…" The Holy Spirit indwelled the prophets of the Old Testament and all believers since Pentecost. Just as the things of God are revealed by the Holy Spirit (1Corinthians 2:12-14), Wisdom reveals the things that please God and lead to salvation (Wisdom 9:18).

Just as God can be found by those who seek Him (Deuteronomy 4:29, 1Chronicles 28:9, 2Chronicles 15:2, Jeremiah 29:13), Wisdom can be found by those who seek Her (Wisdom 6:12). Just as those who love God obey His commands (John 14:21), those who love Wisdom observe Her laws (Wisdom 6:18). Just as Galatians 6:8 promises **"the one who sows to please the Spirit from the Spirit will reap eternal life,"** Wisdom says, "…adherence to her laws is assurance of immortality, and immortality brings men near to God…" (Wisdom 6:18-19, Goodspeed). God gives Wisdom by sending His Holy Spirit from on high (Wisdom 9:17), so their paths on earth were "straightened" (Wisdom 9:18); just as Proverbs 3:5-6 says, **"Trust in the Lord… and he will make your paths straight."** Just as Jesus is the image of God (John 14:9, Colossians 1:15), Wisdom is "…the spotless mirror of the power of God, the image of his goodness" (Wisdom 7:26).

# Comparisons from the Book of Sirach

The Book of Sirach, or Ecclesiasticus, is another apocryphal book written between 200 and 175 BC (7, New American Bible), and also speaks of Wisdom. Genesis 1:2 says, **"…the Spirit of God (Holy Spirit) was hovering over the waters."** Wisdom says, "From the mouth of the Most High I came forth, and mistlike covered the earth" (Sirach 24:3). Sirach 24:4 says, "In the highest heavens did I (Wisdom) dwell, my throne on a pillar of cloud." Exodus 13:21 says that God guided the Israelites in a **"pillar of cloud;"** the same exact words. Sirach 6:28-29 says that if you seek Wisdom, you will find Her and find rest in Her; just as Jesus promises rest to those who come to Him (Matthew 11:28).

Wisdom was created before all things (Sirach 1:4). The Lord himself created her (Sirach 1:7), before all ages (Sirach 24:9), "…and poured her out upon all he made; upon all mankind, as he chose to bestow her; but he supplied her liberally to those who loved him" (Sirach 1:9-10, Goodspeed). *Motherlike*,

Wisdom will nourish and teach him who fears the Lord (Sirach 15:1-3). Those who serve Her serve God, and those who love Her, the LORD loves (Sirach 4:14).

This is an indication as to how God became a triune God. God is infinite, always was and always will be. "In the beginning" God created the heavens and the earth, but before that happened, He "created" Wisdom (or split his essence). He breathed her out (or gave her birth) and She was called the Breath of God. She was the craftsman or helper (Paraclete) at His side.

# Church Fathers

The Apostolic Fathers, or Fathers of the Church, were certain bishops and great Christian teachers who recorded the basic tenets of the Christian faith during the period of about 100 to 600 AD. These writings were used to establish the doctrinal beliefs of the early church and to settle doctrinal disputes.

Clement of Alexandria was a 2nd century leader of the Christian church and wrote:

> And God Himself is love; and out of love to us became feminine. In His ineffable essence He is Father; in His compassion to us He became Mother. The Father by loving became feminine: and the great proof of this is He whom He begot of Himself: and the fruit brought forth by love is love.

*The Ante-Nicene Fathers Volume 6* (3rd and 4th century) discusses the family of Adam, Eve and Seth being a sign or shadow of the Trinity.

> Perhaps these three persons of our ancestors, being in an image the consubstantial repre-

> sentatives of humanity, are, as also Methodius
> thinks, types of the Holy and Consubstantial
> Trinity, the innocent and unbegotten Adam
> being the type and resemblance of God the
> Father Almighty, who is uncaused, and the
> cause of all; his begotten son shadowing forth
> the image of the begotten Son and Word of
> God; whilst Eve, that proceedeth forth from
> Adam, signifies the person and procession of
> the Holy Spirit.

The Gospel of the Hebrews (Gheb) is one of several gospels that were not chosen as part of our Bible and no copy has survived to today. Early Christian writers from the mid-second century to early fifth century quoted the material from this gospel quite often. The only parts of this gospel we have to refer to are the quotes from these early writers. It is believed to have been written in the early second century (8, Miller).

This Gospel of the Hebrews that was quoted by early church fathers depicts the Holy Spirit as feminine and as the mother of Jesus. The Semitic word for "spirit" is feminine in gender. "This distinctive depiction of the spirit is rooted in Jewish speculation about divine Wisdom, a female personification of one of God's attributes who was believed to dwell with 'holy souls'" (9, Miller).

Jerome lived 347 to 420 AD and was considered the most learned scholar of the Fathers of the Roman Church. His greatest achievement was the translation of the Bible from the original languages, mainly Hebrew and Greek, into a Latin version known as the Vulgate. The following is an excerpt from his commentary on the Gospel of the Hebrews.

> 4d Quoted and explained by Jerome, Commentary on Isaiah 11 (commentary on Isa 40:9)

> In the Gospel of the Hebrews that the Nazarenes read it says,
>
> "Just now my mother, the holy spirit, took me." (Jesus speaking)
>
> Now no one should be *offended* by this, because "spirit" in Hebrew is feminine, while in our language (Latin) it is masculine and in Greek it is neuter. In divinity however, there is no gender. (10, Miller, brackets and italics added)

This clearly indicates that Jerome believed the Holy Spirit was the spiritual mother of Christ, the Son of God.

Philo of Alexandria (ca. 20 BC–50 AD) is the most prominent Jewish philosopher of antiquity known to us. He wrote extensive commentaries on scripture and his writings support Jerome's understanding of this relationship within the Trinity. Wisdom was with God before the creation of the world. She was God's spouse and the mother of the created world (11, Schafer).

This truth seems to be evident to serious students of the Bible who seek to find the truth of God and are not willing to accept man's version of that truth. The translators and commentators of the New International Version Study Bible have supported this without actually saying it. In Matthew 11:19, Jesus says, **"…But wisdom is proved right by her actions."** The study note explains *wisdom refers to God*. In Luke 7:35 in the same context, Jesus said, **"But wisdom is proved right by all her children,"** referring to spiritually wise people being the children of God.

> Happy is the man who *meditates* on Wisdom,
> and reflects on knowledge; who ponders her
> ways in his heart, and understands her paths;
> who pursues her like a scout and lies in wait
> at her entry way; ...who takes shelter with
> her from the heat, and dwells in her home.
> He who fears the Lord will do this; he who
> is practiced in the law will come to wisdom.
> *Motherlike* she will meet him, like a young
> bride she will embrace him. Nourish him
> with the *bread* of understanding, and give
> him the *water of learning* to drink. He will
> lean upon her and *not fall*, he will *trust in
> her* and *not be put to shame*. She will *exalt
> him* above his fellows... (Sirach 14:20-15:5,
> italics added)

Scripture admonishes us to seek the Lord and *meditate* on His word day and night. Jesus referred to the Holy Spirit, our teacher, as *living water* (John 7:38). The New Testament describes Jesus as the *bread of life*. We are to humble ourselves before God and He will *exalt* us.

I find it very pertinent that Wisdom, the Holy Spirit, will be like a mother, or a bride, to the person who seeks Her and trusts in Her ways. God offers to be our father and also a husband to those who do not have one.

Wisdom calls:

> *Come to me*, all you that yearn for me, and
> be filled with my *fruits* (Sirach 24:18). Submit
> your neck to *her yoke*, that your mind may ac-
> cept *her teaching*. For she is close to those who
> seek her, and the one who is in earnest finds
> her. (Sirach 51:26-27, italics added)

Jesus says:

> ***Come to me***, **all you who are weary and burdened and I will give you rest. Take *my yoke* upon you and *learn from me*, for I am gentle and humble in heart, and you will find rest for your souls. For *my yoke is easy* and my burden is light. (Matthew 11:28-30, italics added)**

Wisdom, as personified in many writings, is the Holy Spirit; the part of God that indwells all creation and brings Godly counsel and comfort to those who love and embrace the truth of God. It is the Holy Spirit, or Wisdom, who enables us to understand the things of God. The Holy Spirit is the helper who comes alongside and is feminine in nature. Womanhood reflects this essence of the Holy Spirit. It saddens me that this aspect of God has been lost for so long, for as Billy Graham said, we lose the joy and power of God when we do not see Him clearly. A true relationship is based on knowing one another, and this includes a true relationship with our God.

# Notes

1.   Billy Graham, *The Holy Spirit,* (Dallas, TX: Word Publishing, 1988) p. 11.
2.   *New International Version Disciples Study Bible,* (Nashville: Holman Bible Publishers, 1988) p. 7.
3.   Trent C. Butler, Editor, *Holman Bible Dictionary,* (Nashville: Holman Bible Publishers, 1991) p. 1074.
4.   Rebecca Oxford-Carpenter, "Gender and the Trinity," *Theology Today*, Vol. 41, No 1, April, 1984.
5.   Peter Schafer, *Mirror of His Beauty*, (Princeton, NJ: Princeton University Press, 2002) p. 9.
6.   *The New American Bible*, (Canada: World Catholic Press, 1987) p. 680.
7.   *The New American Bible*, p. 699.

8.  Robert J. Miller, Editor, *The Complete Gospels*: *Annotated Scholars Version*, (San Francisco: Harper Collins, 1992) p. 432, 426, 429.

9.  Miller, p. 428.

10. Miller, p. 432.

11. Schafer, p. 39-41.

# Chapter 3

## *Motherhood of God*

### The Apostles Creed

I believe in God the Father Almighty, maker of heaven and earth; and in Jesus Christ His only Son, our Lord; who was conceived by the Holy Spirit, born of the Virgin Mary...

### The Nicene Creed

I believe in one God the Father Almighty, Maker of Heaven and earth, and of all things visible and invisible: and in one Lord Jesus Christ, the only–begotten Son of God, begotten of His Father before all worlds, God of God, Light of Light, very God of Very God, begotten, not made, being of one substance with the Father...

Jesus Christ is the begotten son of the Father God, not made or created. Speakers and writers today say that Jesus was conceived by the Holy Spirit, born of the Virgin Mary. They leave out God, the Father's role; two coming together to produce a son of their own substance. This is stated clearly in Luke, but overlooked today.

The angel, Gabriel, came to Mary to tell her she would give birth to the Son of God, and she asked how this could happen when she was a virgin (Luke 1:31-34). **"The angel answered, 'The Holy Spirit will come upon you, and the power of the *Most High* will overshadow you. So the holy one to be born will be called the Son of God'" (Luke 1:35, italics added).** The Holy Spirit *and the Father God*, referred to 58 times in scripture as Most High, were both involved in the physical conception of the incarnate Jesus in the womb of the Virgin Mary. The begotten Son of God (the Word) was "begotten of His Father *before all worlds*" (before the creation of the world and man), "...begotten, not made, being of one substance with the Father." (Nicene Creed, italics and parenthesis added). He was also "...conceived by the Holy Spirit," (Apostolic Creed).

The Father God is the father of Jesus and the Holy Spirit is the spiritual mother of Jesus. This could explain why, in scripture, Jesus never referred to Mary as mother. He called her "woman" (John 2:4, John 19:26). Just as Adam called Eve, woman, bone of my bone and flesh of my flesh. Jesus was referring to the physical relationship between Himself and Mary.

Other than Wisdom referring to her sons, the Holy Spirit is never called the mother of believers in the Bible, but the nature of this relationship is clearly inferred. **"...no one can enter the kingdom of God unless he is born of water and the Spirit" (John 3:5). "So it is with everyone born of the Spirit" (John 3:8). "For you have been born again," (Peter 1:23). "No one who is born of God will continue to sin, because God's seed remains in him..." (1 John 3:9). "Every one who believes that Jesus is the Christ is born of God, and everyone who loves the Father loves his child as well" (1 John 5:1). "...you forgot the God who gave you birth"**

(**Deuteronomy 32:18**). Believers are born of the Spirit, and are also children of God.

The feminine and mothering qualities of God have been suppressed over time; whether completely intentional or not, I cannot say. I believe part of the reason could be an overreaction to idolatrous female goddesses and Mariolatry, the divination of Mary by the Roman Catholic Church. Scripture clearly reveals these qualities of God, but does not attribute them to the Holy Spirit.

> **Can a mother forget the baby at her breast and have no compassion on the child she has borne? Though she may forget, I will not forget you! (Isaiah 49:15)**

> **As a mother comforts her child, so I (God) will comfort you… (Isaiah 66:13 parenthesis added)**

> **I have longed to gather your children together, as a hen gathers her chicks under her wings…" (Jesus said in Matthew 23:37 and in Luke 13:34 about the people of Jerusalem.)**

As previously mentioned, El-Shaddai, God Almighty, means full-breasted. In Luke 15:8-10, Jesus relays how important it is for God to save every person by describing a woman who lost a coin and tore her home apart to find it.

An eagle, or bird in general, is often used to describe the care God provides His children. As early as Genesis 1:2, the Spirit of God is said to hover over the waters, similar to a bird protecting its young. In the Song of Moses, he compares the care of God to a mother eagle that stirs up her nest and hovers over her young and carries them on her pinions, or wings

(Deuteronomy 32:11). Many verses in Psalms speak of taking refuge in the shadow or shelter of God's wings, or being carried on His wings. In Exodus 19:3, God tells Moses how He carried the Israelites on eagles wings and brought them to Himself. These are all nurturing qualities of God that are feminine in nature.

Revelation is a book I have not studied in depth, but I found chapter 12 very pertinent when looking at the motherhood of God. It speaks of a woman clothed with the sun (fire). She was about to give birth to a son who would rule all the nations with an iron scepter. Revelation 12:5, 19:15 and Psalm 2:9 all refer to Christ ruling with an iron scepter. Satan was waiting to devour her child. Before he could, the child (named as Christ in the NAS) was snatched up to God and His throne. **"Christ, the first born of all creation and by him all things were created." (Colossians 1:15).** In John 17, Jesus refers to this time with the Father when they shared glory before the world was and when the Father loved Him before the foundation (creation) of the world.

After the birth of Christ, the woman was given wings like those of a great *eagle* to escape with. Satan was enraged and he **"went off to make war against the *rest of her offspring*— those who obey God's commands and hold to the testimony of Jesus" (Rev 12:17 italics added).** This is a clear picture of the spiritual birth of Christ whose mother is represented by fire and as a bird, both symbols of the Holy Spirit. She is also the mother of believers whom Satan is warring against.

Isaiah also speaks of the spiritual birth of Christ. **"The LORD called Me from the womb; from the body of My mother He named Me and He has made My mouth like a sharp sword; (Isaiah 49:1-2 NAS).**

Begotten, not created, of the same substance as God. Jesus is the Son of God the Father and of this female entity that is the Holy Spirit! We, as believers in Jesus, through our spiritual birth, are the children of God, the sons and daughters of God the Father, but also the "offspring" of the Holy Spirit.

With time, Christian writers and theologians have eliminated the spiritual mother and the feminine quality of this spiritual relationship. Jerome indicated some would be "offended" by this aspect of God and how His different qualities work in our personal lives. It is time this truth of God is brought back into our understanding of who God is. This promotion of a totally male God has devalued women, not only in society, but also in their own eyes. Jesus said we must worship in spirit and in truth. This falsehood must also hurt the cause of Christianity in ways we cannot even comprehend.

Oswald Chambers was a great Christian writer and teacher of the early 1900's. His teachings and sermons have been compiled into *My Utmost for His Highest*, the most widely read daily devotional ever published, and several Christian classics. In *Christian Disciplines*, he explains the nature of the Holy Spirit and how knowing and understanding the nature of God enables us to reach the true goal of life—God Himself. Oswald Chambers was very much aware of the role of women and womanhood in God's plan for the redemption of mankind. He also recognized the Holy Spirit as feminine and as the spiritual mother of believers.

> In this connection it is of importance to note that the Bible reveals that our Redeemer entered into the world through the woman. Man, as man, had no part whatsoever in the Redemption of the world; it was "the seed of the woman."
> All that we understand by womanhood and by manhood, all that we understand by fatherhood and motherhood, is embraced in the term El Shaddai (Genesis 17:1, 19). (1, Chambers)

I will pray the Father, and He will give you another Helper, that He may abide with you forever—the Spirit of truth, whom the world cannot receive, because it neither sees Him nor knows him; but you know Him, for He dwells with you and will be in you. I will not leave you orphans; I will come to you. (John 16-18)

Call the Helper by the term you think best— Advocate, Comforter, Paraclete, the word conveys the indefinable blessedness of His sympathy—an inward, invisible kingdom that causes the saint to sing through every night of sorrow. This Holy Comforter represents the ineffable motherhood of God. Protestantism has lost for many generations this aspect of the divine revelation because of its violent antipathy to Mariolatry as practiced by the Roman Catholic Church: and it behooves us to remember that Protestantism is not the whole gospel of God, but an expression of a view of the gospel God specially adapted to the crying needs of a particular time.

George MacDonald in his book entitled *Sir Gibbie*, writes as follows...:

> See revelation culminate in Elizabeth and Mary, the mothers of John the Baptist and Jesus. Think how much fitter that it should be so; that they to whom the Word of God comes

should be women bred in the dignity of a natural life, and familiarity with the large ways of the earth; women of simple and few wants, without distraction, and with time for reflection—compelled to reflection, indeed, from the enduring presence of an unsullied consciousness, for wherever there is a humble, thoughtful nature, into that nature the divine consciousness, that is, the Spirit of God, presses as into its own place.

We quote this simply for the purpose of suggesting how we limit ourselves and our concept of God by ignoring the side of the divine nature best symbolized by womanhood, and the Comforter, be it reverently said, surely represents this side of the divine nature. It is the Comforter who sheds abroad the love of God in our hearts. It is the Comforter who baptizes us into oneness with Jesus, in the amazing language of Scripture, until we are indwelled by a mysterious union with God. It is the Comforter who brings forth the fruit of love, joy, peace, long-suffering, kindness, goodness, faithfulness, meekness, temperance. Guidance by His sympathy leads by a blessed discipline into an understanding of God which passes knowledge. (2, Chambers)

I have often reflected on the difference in the way men and women respond to God and His call to them. Traditionally, pastors and leaders of churches have been men, and it also seems the man is to be the spiritual leader of the home. However, it appears to me that women in general have stronger faith and are more active in the church than men. They seem to be more spiritual and open to the mysteries of God. Could this be because of their God-given feminine natures that recognize the nature of the Holy Spirit?

Father God is portrayed as the leader, provider, protector, rule maker and disciplinarian. The Old Testament is dominated by God the Father. It is focused on the law, the activity of worship and discipline as a consequence of disobedience. Jesus came to initiate a new covenant, a covenant of grace and love to replace the old covenant of law, and it is the Holy Spirit who facilitates this covenant.

This amazing plan of God for mankind's relationship with Him is also reflected in the nature of man. Man is a triune being just as God is. He is body (physical), soul (mind, emotion and will) and spirit. God's interaction with mankind has been triune. The Old Testament was a physical, external relationship. Man, as servant, was to follow the law and live and worship in obedience to God's rules to win favor with Him.

When the time was right (in the fullness of time,) God sent His son in a physical body to intercede and provide a way for us to become children of God, to enter into the family of God. Jesus came and taught mankind about the Kingdom of God. He explained, He did miracles and He set an example as to how to enter this Kingdom. This was a "soul" work. This was striving to change the minds of men and women, so they could "understand" what the kingdom of God is. Today we can renew our minds by reading and hearing the words of Christ.

But no matter how much soul or mind work we do, we cannot come to know God unless our spirits are born of the Spirit of God (born again). Jesus said we must be born of water and the Spirit to enter the Kingdom of God (John 3:5). When we are converted by the Holy Spirit, or born again, our spirits are cleansed and freed of sin and we become righteous in the eyes of God.

To live a godly life pleasing to God, we have to combine these two processes. We must experience a new (spiritual) birth that makes us spiritually clean and part of God's family. At this time we receive the gift of faith from God. Then we need to renew our minds through the washing of the word so our physical bodies can live a life that produces fruit for the Kingdom of God. This fruit flows out of our works. This is the abundant life Jesus speaks of.

When Jesus finished His work, giving His life for the redemption of mankind, He returned to the Father and they sent the Spirit to fulfill the next part of God's plan. She came at Pentecost in a mighty and powerful way, indwelling believers and empowering them to build the Church of Christ.

Jesus is the head of the Church, or the Body of Christ. He guides the actions of the Church. Just as He came to convince us how to live in a way that is pleasing to God, He is still leading us to live in a godly manner doing godly work. This is still the work of the mind. But it is only by the presence and power of the Holy Spirit that this work can be accomplished. She is the comforter, helper, counselor, teacher and nurturer it takes to build a relationship with God and relationships within the Church.

This quality of the Holy Spirit and Her connection to womanhood is new to most Christians and not accepted as mainstream Christian teaching. The motivation is unclear, but it was deliberately left out of early Christian writings and has been lost with time.

I believe the Queen of Heaven is another part of this unknown truth of God. This term has been used to describe pagan goddesses and the Roman church has given this designation to the Virgin Mary. I consider these both to be completely erroneous and that the true Queen of Heaven is the Holy

Spirit. She is the woman in Revelation who gave birth to the Messiah and wore a crown with twelve stars.

Just as the truth of the Reformation, or Protestantism, was God's answer to the need of a particular time, I believe this is the time this truth about the nature of the Holy Spirit needs to be revealed. She is the Spirit of Truth and truth will always win out. We cannot expect the blessing of a God who values truth when we are suppressing it. It is time our Christian leaders do what is necessary to promote a clearer picture of who God is, including the feminine nature and role of the Holy Spirit.

I believe there is a longing in women's hearts to become aware of this aspect of God. Having a more truthful image of God would open the spirits of people to receive the one true God. As this truth changes the status and well being of women around the world, it will also improve the condition of our hurting families.

There is so much to learn about God, and each one of us has to take that individual journey of coming to know Him as He truly is. True peace and contentment in this life are found in having an accurate understanding of who God is, including the feminine qualities of God expressed by the Holy Spirit. This leads to finding the purpose for which we were created and the Kingdom "work" that we are ideally suited to do. This journey is the adventure of a lifetime and it takes a lifetime to experience it.

# Notes

1. Taken from *Biblical Psychology* by Oswald Chambers, © 1962 by the Oswald Chambers Publications Assn., Ltd., p. 25. Used by permission of Discovery House Publishers, Grand Rapids, MI 49501. All rights reserved.
2. Taken from *Christian Disciplines* by Oswald Chambers, © 1936, 1995 by the Oswald Chambers Publications Assn., Ltd., P. 34-36. Used by permission of Discovery House Publishers, Grand Rapids, MI 49501. All rights reserved.

# Chapter 4

## *God's Design*

There is so much wisdom and insight in the Bible. It was inspired by the almighty Most High God, our creator. He knows us better than we know ourselves. He knows what motivates our behavior and what brings us peace and contentment. How much time have we spent striving for what we thought would make us happy, but, when acquired, did not? We need to realize that it is only God and His purpose for our lives that will bring us the "abundant" life He promises. Abundance does not mean lots of "stuff," nor happiness in every area of our lives. To me it means a full, complete life that has purpose and spiritual peace, peace of the soul. God brings us happiness and joy in some areas, but conflict and strife in other areas to mature and change us; to make us more like Jesus. This is a life long process.

The question is how do we approach life? Do we accept that the God who created us wants us to enjoy a life that is full and rich? If we do, we accept that He has told us how we can find that life in scripture.

**...man does not live on bread alone but on every word that comes from the mouth of the LORD. (Deuteronomy 8:3)**

**All Scripture is God-breathed and is useful for teaching, rebuking, correcting and training in righteousness, so that the man of God may be thoroughly equipped for every good work. (2Timothy 3:16-17)**

By studying scripture, we come to an understanding of who God is and what the true nature of man is. Genesis holds the key to the relationship between God and mankind and our purpose here on earth. The Old Testament is a history of the Israelites and how God dealt with them through obedience and disobedience. It also prophesied the coming of the Messiah as the path of reconciliation to God after the disobedience in the Garden. The New Testament offers us salvation, shows us how to have an intimate relationship with God as our Father and explains how we are to live with those around us.

A theme that runs all through scripture is that of authority and submission. It seems to be the oil that God's kingdom runs on. Only when we recognize and accept God's authority over us, do we enter into lives that "work;" that produce good, right results. All through scripture, God asks us to submit to His ways and plans. When we do, we find peace and joy-filled lives.

The kingdom of God is different from the physical world where physical power seems to rule. God's kingdom runs on His power, and we only access that through submission to Him and His ways. Jesus is our example of this. He came in meekness, but with great strength. He submitted His life to God's purpose for Him on earth. He was even willing to give His life, but in that process, He changed the world forever. He said it is in weakness that God's power can be revealed. It is also in weakness that tyranny is exposed. When we give up trying to control situations, and trust them to God (seek His face and His hand,) we see His power at work.

Do not think I am promoting "religion." I understand the need for Christian fellowship and appreciate that "iron sharpens iron." I am just now coming to understand the value and power in being an active part of the "body of Christ." But, I am also very aware there have been terrible wrongs committed in the name of God. There are many people involved in religious activities that are motivated by self-interest rather than God-interest. If we spend time in His word and develop an intimate relationship with God, He gives us spiritual discernment and a longing for what is true. Finding the truth of God leads us into a life of freedom and abundance.

God created mankind to fellowship with Him, to glorify Him and to populate and care for the earth. If we look closely at the creation, one of the most prominent factors we see is the order involved. God ordained or established the heavens and the earth and all that is in them. The words ordain and order have the same origin. If we look at the heavens and nature, we see His order. The human body is a miraculous example of His order. He instructs us to have order in our behavior, order in our worship and order in our families. When we find chaos, we can be sure God is not the head of the situation.

Order is nowhere more evident than in God's creation of mankind. He created the heavenly Kingdom where there is order and structure. He then created the physical world as a reflection of that spiritual world. He created man in His image, but physical to inhabit the physical world. Paul said in Romans 1:18-20 that man has no excuse for not knowing God for He made the world as a reflection of His nature (triune) and power.

Both of these orderly worlds run on authority and submission. In the heavenly realm, God the Father is the ultimate authority. Both the Holy Spirit and His Son respond to His direction. They are equal to Him in value, but He has the plan of action. When Satan rebelled against that authority, there was war, or chaos. God separated Satan from His kingdom to restore the order.

The Trinity is such an important part of understanding man's creation and the nature of man. **"Then God said, 'Let us make man in our own image, in our likeness…'" (Genesis 1:26).** His image refers to His essence, or nature, while His likeness refers to His function, or role. The three persons of the Trinity, God the Father, God the Holy Spirit and God the Son, are equal in value, but different in function. There is no vying for power or position. They work together to accomplish a *common goal*.

God the Father is the authority, the planner, the rule maker and the disciplinarian. He shows His love to mankind by provision, protection and disciplining when necessary. God the Holy Spirit seems to be the powerful enabler, the entity that plays an active part in carrying out the Father's plan and indwells all creation. She is relational, drawing people into a relationship with the Father and Jesus. She shows Her love for mankind by Her nurturing, counseling and comforting qualities. She is our teacher who draws us into God's plan, giving us a desire to participate in growing the family of God.

After Adam and Eve sinned in the garden, there was a separation between God and man. Jesus, God the Son, was sent by the Father to enable mankind to return to communion with the Father. **"…I do exactly what my Father has commanded me" (John 14:31).** The Son is equal to the Father, but the Father has authority over the actions of the Son. This is the ultimate example of choosing to be submissive. Jesus could have disobeyed God's plan, but He chose to be obedient. He said, **"…yet not my will but yours be done" (Luke 22:42).** After the resurrection, God sent the Holy Spirit to indwell believers and to empower them to live a Christian life.

In heaven, there is God the Father, God the Holy Spirit (or helper of the Father, craftsman at His side), and God the begotten Son of the Father and the Holy Spirit. Each knows his purpose and together creates a unit where harmony is clearly evident. We can look to this relationship to get an idea of God's desire for the family unit on earth. **"For this reason, I bow my knees before the Father, from whom every family in heaven and on earth derives its name (nature)…" (Ephesians 3:14-15, NAS, parentheses added).** God knows it is not possible to have two entities in the same position, so he gave men and women different strengths so that when they come together, embracing each other's unique qualities, they create a strong unit. This results in a family that is functioning in a healthy productive way. Each member is valued and appreciated for who they are and what they bring to the unit.

I have heard this plan described as similar to a military command. There can only be one in charge, but he could not do his job without the second in command. The one in charge collects information and recommendations from the second in command, makes decisions and delegates activities to accomplish goals. If anything goes wrong, he is held accountable. God intends each one of us to put our relationship with Him first, but on earth, it appears the chain of command is God, husband, wife, and children. This authority is not based on greater worth or even ability, but on the need for order in the family. 1Corinthians 11 says God is the head of Christ just as the husband is the head of the wife. In both cases they are equal in value, but there is a difference in roles.

In Ephesians, Paul talks about the marriage relationship and says it is a profound mystery. **"Be imitators of God,"** he says, and goes on to compare the relationship of Christ and the Church to husbands and wives. Jesus submitted to the Father and His plan of salvation for mankind. He became flesh and died on the cross so man could come back into fellowship with

God. Believers together form the body of Christ. He is the head and He gave up His life for the body.

In a similar way, men are to submit to Christ and give up their lives for their wives. They are to love them and care for them as they care for their own bodies. Women are to submit to their husbands and respect them, just as we (the Church) are to submit to God and show Him reverence. It is through this process that we learn to be more like Christ. In the act of submission and giving up our lives, we emulate Christ and what He did for mankind. We also participate in God's goal of creating godly offspring, both physical children and also spiritual believers.

When this godly pattern is displayed in a physical family, children and other observers get a glimpse of the workings of the spiritual kingdom.

The world would refer to this as a doormat mentality, but there was obviously no doormat mentality on Jesus' part. It took great strength and determination to carry out the Father's plan, but He knew the glory it would lead to and the blessing it would be for mankind.

In *"It's How We Are Wired,"* Alex McFarland recently explained that God's intent for men, women and marriage is a reflection of the order of the Godhead, and that we can understand important truths about God by studying these relationships. Father, Son and Holy Spirit are equal in value, but each member performs unique functions. These are inherent truths that cannot be disregarded by cultural changes.

Rick Warren in *The Purpose Driven Life* expressed similar ideas:

> Because God is love, he treasures relationships. His very nature is relational, and he identifies himself in family terms: Father, Son, and Spirit. The Trinity is God's relationship to himself. It's the perfect pattern

for relational harmony, and we should study its implications. (1, Warren)

Paul quoted the Old Testament and said, **"For this reason a man will leave his father and mother and be united to his wife, and the two will become one flesh." This is a profound mystery—but I am talking about Christ and the Church (Ephesians 5:31-32).** Malachi 2:15 goes on to explain this is because God is seeking godly offspring. When the husband, a shadow or type of Jesus submits to the authority of God, and the wife, a shadow or type of the church, submits to her husband, the order of God's plan is displayed. This not only results in a healthy home where godly children can be raised, but it also opens the way for the blessing and power of God to flow through this family to those around them. Malachi also explains this is why God hates divorce. It splits apart what He has joined together; breaking a family and creating chaos that hurts children.

There is much speculation on what Paul meant when he said, **"…the unbelieving husband has been sanctified through his wife, and the unbelieving wife has been sanctified through her believing husband…" (1 Corinthians 7:14).** He was not talking about our salvation, he was referring to God's desire for us to raise godly children. The unbelieving spouse (unclean) is made clean (sanctified) by the believing spouse so that their children can be clean. **"…otherwise your children would be unclean, but as it is, they are holy" (1Corinthians 7:14).**

God instructed mankind to populate and care for the earth. **"God blessed *them* and said to *them*…" (Genesis 1:28, italics added).** God spoke to both Adam and Eve together appointing them *partners* in the task. Eve's primary concern was the family and procreation, while Adam's was caring for the earth as he protected and provided for the family. In the Garden of Eden, this was an easy task. There was no toiling or labor involved. Because of Adam and Eve's disobedience to God, they were expelled from the garden, just as Satan was expelled from God's presence. This also included the receiving of a sin nature. **"...sin entered the world..." (Romans 5:12).** Our natural, human tendencies are the result of the fall and are constantly in conflict with our spiritual natures.

> **To the woman he said, "I will greatly increase your pains in childbearing; with pain you will give birth to children. Your desire will be for your husband, and he will rule over you." (Genesis 3:16)**

> **To Adam he said, "Because you listened to your wife and ate from the tree about which I commanded you, 'You must not eat of it,' "Cursed is the ground because of you; through painful toil you will eat of it all the days of your life. It will produce thorns and thistles for you, and you will eat the plants of the field. By the sweat of your brow you will eat your food until you return to the ground, since from it you were taken; for dust you are and to dust you will return." (Genesis 3:17-19)**

The consequences of their sin were reflected in their most basic roles on earth. The woman was to have difficulty and more pain in childbirth. The man, as the provider and protector, would labor to work the soil. It is interesting that the word "labor" describes the consequences of both the man and woman's disobedience.

Their relationship would also be greatly affected. God told Eve, **"...Your desire will be for your husband, and he will rule over you" (Genesis 3:16).** The Hebrew word used here for desire has the element of control in it and can be understood as the woman will desire to control her husband and the husband has the tendency to rule over and subdue his wife. By being aware of what our basic human nature is, we can strive to behave in a way that is motivated by unselfishness and love. Both husband and wife are to submit to each other (Ephesians 5:21) to overcome these tendencies that are ungodly and harmful to the relationship. This leads to putting the needs of the family before personal desires. This is a picture of agape, or unconditional love.

The physical qualities of a man's body clearly enable him to be the provider and protector of the family. Except for the industrialization of some countries over the past 100 years, provision was and is acquired by physical strength. God made him physically stronger than the woman because He knew he would have to work the ground to provide food for the family, and knowing the nature of man, would have to protect the family from outsiders.

Man is called to be the head of the family, but the woman is the heart. God created her, not only to bear children, but also to build the home. He gave her a gentleness and softness that would enable her to nurture children, and also to comfort and care for her husband. Man was to build the house; but woman was to build the home, creating an extension of the womb, a place of nurturing and love that children need to develop healthily. God created woman for relationships, giving her feelings and emotions that strengthen her need for intimate interaction with her family, especially her husband. He created man with a need for physical intimacy that can only be found in a close, loving relationship.

Even though God gave this aspect of marital strife as a result of sin, the basic needs He created in us are still there. Jimmy Evans in *Marriage on the Rock* says a man's most basic needs are first respect and then physical intimacy, whereas a woman's are security and non-physical affection.

A man's world is more physical, requiring a sexually intimate relationship to fulfill his needs of respect and completeness; whereas a woman needs emotional intimacy to feel secure and valued. A healthy relationship based on unselfish love requires the husband to desire to provide for and protect his wife, even when she has the ability to meet those needs herself. He needs to embrace the importance of emotional interaction with his wife, even though it does not come naturally to him. The wife needs to respect her husband and support him as he provides for the family. She also needs to understand his physical needs, accepting that they are different from hers. This creates a bond and a dependency that not only builds a strong satisfying relationship, but also helps marriages survive difficult times. God knew the survival of mankind depended on these most basic needs that can only be met by the opposite sex.

I continue to be not only amazed but also truly awed by God's creation. He did not stop with these obvious differences between men and women. Our total beings support these basic differences. A man's brain, because of hormone changes in the womb, forms in a different way than a woman's. We truly think differently and it promotes a difference that when joined together, enhances the partnership.

Because of these physical differences in the development of the brain, men tend to think with one side of the brain at a time, where as women are processing information from both sides at once. This allows a man to intensely focus on the situation at hand, shutting out distractions, whereas a woman is taking lots of information into consideration at once. A man is created to act. He comes at a problem with his mind, logic and goal achieving the priority. A woman comes at a problem with her heart and emotions affecting her decisions. This is not to say a woman cannot use logic or that a man cannot consider emotions, but our immediate and dominant reaction to a situation follows these tendencies.

One way is not better than the other, but there are *situations* where one is better than the other. This mental quality enables men to go out into the world and shut out personal concerns that interfere with getting their jobs done. When they get home, they need to make a conscious transition from that work role to the role of husband and father. Women are programmed to handle the variety of jobs and emotions it takes to care for a husband, run a household and nurture children all at the same time. If they work outside the home, they tend to take personal issues to work with them and need to make more of an effort to focus on work. As I have said, one is not better than the other. Even in the workplace, there are jobs that demand one style of thinking over the other. This is one reason some professions are dominated by one sex or the other.

I have often wondered if this is why historically men have predominately been the inventors and artists. The ability to section brain activity and subdue those areas not needed for a function would enhance and emphasize the activity of the area being used. This seems similar to a person who loses a sense. For example, a person's sense of hearing, touch and smell is sensitized when he has lost the sense of sight.

I have heard men say that they always consult their wives when making judgments or decisions. They realize their wives are more sensitive and aware of a broader, or possibly just different, range of information. Women see things from a different perspective and also see details the husband can miss. This is often called intuition. A woman can come to an accurate conclusion and not be able to give a reason why. They say they feel it, which is the result of taking in details they are not consciously aware of.

In most marriages and families, these differences cause conflict and chaos. It is not easy to embrace the fact that we think differently. If something is important to me, I naturally think it should be important to everyone else. When these differences are understood and valued, it is possible to draw on the strength and unique perspective of both to create a strong family unit.

You may be thinking this was fine for Bible times, but not for today. Women are educated, independent and often smarter than their husbands. However, the wise woman will consider this admonition of scripture and even test it. 1Peter 3 says that when a woman is responding correctly to her husband, she has great influence over him, even winning an unbeliever to Christ. God is pleased with her obedience to Him and blesses the whole family because of the heart of the woman. Of course, God would not expect a woman to be submissive to physical abuse or things He has said in His word are wrong. There are times a woman has to take a stand against her husband if he is thinking wrong or making a mistake.

I have searched scripture to find clues as to how a woman today can live this balancing act of being a strong, wise woman and still obedient to this role God has given her. On the one hand, 1Peter 3:4-5 explains we are to make ourselves beautiful and of great worth to God by having a gentle and quiet spirit and by being submissive to our husbands. The Proverbs wife of noble character is a strong woman who loves the LORD, but she is also very busy caring for her family and for the poor. She works, she buys, sells and she plans for the future. She treats her husband with respect and brings him honor.

On the other hand, I also found examples of women who went against their husbands and were rewarded by God. Abigail went against her husband who refused to give provisions to David and his men. She not only saved her household, but, after her husband's death, she became David's wife (1Samuel 25). God was going to kill Moses for refusing to have his son circumcised and Zipporah, his wife, had to do it (Exodus 4:24-26). In both cases, the wives knew what God expected and they acted to protect their families.

When Ananias lied to God and was killed, his wife, Sapphira, could have told the truth and lived, but she followed her husbands lead and died (Acts 5:1-11).

Scripture also explains that when a husband loves his wife sacrificially, as Jesus loves the church, he cleanses her and makes her holy. This somehow empowers her and gives her wisdom. This process develops healthy couples, families and children.

This plan only works when the motivation behind it is love and the good of the other person and the family overall. Submission and giving up one's life for another are both choices that go against our human nature. If we want healthy marriages and children, we must be willing to turn away from selfish desires and focus on what is good for the family unit. This can only be accomplished when one has submitted their life to God.

> "For the husband is head of the wife, as also Christ is head of the church." If Christ is the Head of the husband, he is easily the head of the wife, not by effort, but because of the nature of the essentially feminine. But if Jesus Christ is not the Head of the husband, the husband is not the head of the wife. Our Lord always touches the most sacred human relationships, and He says—You must be right with Me first before those relationships can be right; (2, Chambers)

My conclusion about relationships within the family is this: husband and wife are of equal value, but God has given them different qualities and strengths. The husband answers to God for the health of his family, but in accomplishing this, he seeks his wife's counsel in areas in which she is stronger. There is a clear picture in my mind of a healthy couple. They do not stand side by side. They stand back to back, supporting and protecting each other, especially in weak areas. The man faces out to the world and the woman faces in to the family. They need each other, not only to survive, but also to have healthy, productive relationships within the family.

The perfect example of this in scripture is Joseph and Mary. God sent His angel to Mary to tell her about her pregnancy and the Messiah. He told her about Elizabeth being pregnant and as a result, Mary went to her. She received confirmation of what the angel had told her, and she also experienced Elizabeth's birth process to help her when her time came. These are all mothering, relational, family matters.

God sent His angel to Joseph several times with messages of provision and protection. Because Joseph obeyed the angel's messages, Mary and Jesus were in the right place at the right time and were also provided for and protected from those who would harm the Christ child. These are responsibilities given to men.

When Adam and Eve sinned in the Garden, Adam was held responsible. God gave directives to Adam and it was Adam's responsibility to protect Eve. **"When the woman saw that the fruit of the tree was good for food and pleasing to the eye, and also desirable for gaining wisdom, she took some and ate it. She also gave some to her husband, *who was with her*, and he ate it" (Genesis 3:6 italics added).** This is an indication that Adam stood by and did not try to stop Eve from disobeying God.

> There was no conscious intention to disobey in Eve's heart, she was deceived by the cunning wisdom of Satan via the serpent. Adam, however, was not deceived, he sinned with a deliberate understanding of what he was doing; so the Bible associates "sin" with Adam ("Therefore, just as through one man sin en-

> tered into the world…"—Romans 5:12) and
> "transgression" with Eve ("And Adam was
> not deceived, but the woman being deceived
> fell into the transgression"—1Timothy 2:14).
> (3, Chambers)

If we look at this closely, we get insight into another area of the nature of men and women. Eve was more deceivable than Adam, but Adam followed Eve's lead. Women have great influence over men. Adrian Rogers compared a woman's influence on a man as a wind on fire. A wind can fan a fire into a blaze or it can put it out. The saying that behind every successful man is a strong, or wise, woman comes from this influence women have. She has great influence, not only over her husband, but also her children. She can build a sense of security and self-worth in both her husband and children they can receive nowhere else. A woman rightly related to God has great power for good in her family and on her society. Conversely, a woman unaware of these things can do serious harm to her family.

> "The one who hauls you nearer to God may
> be your mother or wife or sweetheart. If a
> woman's life is essentially related to God, her
> whole life is a sacrament for God; if not, her
> life may be a sacrament for the devil." (4,
> Chambers)

As previously mentioned, Scripture truly is amazing. When we need a simple answer to a simple problem, it can be found there. But it also has many levels and depths to it. God has revealed human nature to us in scripture, but it is not always explained in a way that is easy to see. When God lead the Israelites into the Promised Land, one of His stipulations was not to marry foreign wives or take them for their sons. He did not say why. He just said it and expected the Israelites to know He had their best interests in mind and He was not just restricting their pleasure.

There are many references to situations of men marrying foreign wives, women who were not raised in a Hebrew home and did not know God. They lead their men into idolatry and destruction. They did not raise godly children. God knew the strengths and weaknesses of both sexes and gave them commands that would result in healthy families and a strong relationship with Him. When mankind ignores God's directives, it leads to destruction, both in their families and their nations.

> **Then to Adam He said, "Because you have listened to the voice of your wife…" (Genesis 3:17 NAS)**

> **…Abram listened to the voice of Sarai. (Genesis 16:2 NAS)**

Both of these instances in Scripture lead to disobedience and not trusting God, and the results were disastrous.

Of course, the influence of the man on the wife and family is as profound. He is the first in command and God gives the plan for the family to him. He is the steady rock the family needs to be founded on. For the marriage and family to be healthy, he must be willing and able to provide, not only physical needs, but also a healthy emotional partnership with his wife. His involvement with sons and daughters is especially important in raising emotionally stable, productive children. He is the leader who sets the example and determines the course they will take. He must be willing to stand up for what is right and protect his family from any influence that is not good for the family as a whole. This includes being firm when he needs to say no to a wife making poor decisions.

When God separated Adam into male and female, He purposefully gave them strengths and weaknesses that required them to cleave together to create a strong family unit. Because a woman is strong in the heart/relational area, she needs protection in the mental/behavioral area. Since a man is more reasoning/physical, he needs protection in the heart/relational area. True love includes striving to protect our spouses in their weak areas.

Until recently, the physical differences between men and women—the physical strength of men and the child bearing responsibilities of women—have generally determined the position of men and women in the family and in society. Men have had power and control over women and have run society. In general, this power has been abused, and families and society have suffered from this.

This suppression of women and their feelings of worth have caused them to rebel. Not finding pleasure and fulfillment in their homes, they have gone too far the other way, demanding the same status as men, wanting the same things men have.

The women's liberation movement of the 1960s and 70s promoted freedom and independence for women by demanding equal treatment. It promoted the idea that women are the same as men. One of the outcomes was the sexual revolution. This movement supported the idea that sexual freedom leads to equality between the sexes. The sad thing is that while women thought they were winning equality and freedom, they were actually giving up their power and influence. This has allowed men to have casual sex without responsibilities. Women wonder why men will not commit to marriage. Many men just want the benefits of marriage and not the responsibilities. This leaves them free to walk away from a relationship and those responsibilities at any time. Women are also leaving basically good marriages because they think there is something better for them. With time, they find themselves in a similar situation, or even a worse one.

I believe this movement has backfired on both women and society. It has resulted in less marriage and a higher divorce rate that leaves children and women suffering financially, emotionally and physically. Children are growing up in homes without their fathers, and generally, mothers are bearing a larger portion of the financial and parenting burden. I believe this is the cause of many of our problems in society today. Crime, drug use, child abuse and suicide are all higher in broken families. This is a cycle that feeds on itself. Children from broken families have a harder time creating healthy families.

2Peter 2 talks about false teachers that lead people away from the truth. We have allowed the voice of our society to do the same thing. **"…by appealing to the lustful desires of sinful human nature, they entice people who are just escaping from those who live in error. They promise them freedom, while they themselves are slaves of depravity—for a man is slave to whatever has mastered him"** (2Peter 2:18-19).

This may be hard for some people to hear, but it is evident that these problems stem from sexual immorality. Men have denied the need for physical restraint, and women bought in to the lie that free sex was some how freeing. Instead, it has imprisoned mothers and women in singleness and the heartaches that leads to. It laid a foundation that has lead to casual sex, even children having sex indiscriminately. It has lead to higher rates of divorce, unwed mothers, rampant STDs, abortion and an exploding pornography industry.

The terrible thing is that the younger generation has accepted casual sex as the norm. Children grow up bombarded with messages from the media, family, friends and even their schools that say sex is okay as long as it is "safe" sex. Many of our children are harmed for life before they are even old enough to make wise decisions about sex.

This is a reflection of what happened in the garden with Adam and Eve. Satan tempted Eve with something God told her to stay away from. She was deceived into *thinking* it would be a good thing and took it. Adam stood by, did not protect her and *followed her lead*, knowing it was harmful; thus allowing his family to fall into corruption.

God knew the importance of physical intimacy and the result of its abuse. That is why there are so many warnings in scripture against sex outside of marriage. They are not there to restrict us or deny us pleasure. They are there for the good of mankind. When God said cleave to one another forsaking all others, He was expressing the importance of both physical exclusivity and emotional intimacy in marriage.

If we look at societies down through history, we see a repeated pattern. The ones that advanced in power and influence eventually accepted casual sex as the norm. This was the result of turning away from God and His directives and allowing natural tendencies to rule behavior. Scripture says that with the increase of knowledge, each man will do what is right in his own eyes. Today, we are too accepting of basing decisions on our desires and what feels right. This always leads to the breakdown of families, the devaluing of life and the destruction of societies.

God saw that it was not good that Adam was alone, so He gave him a companion and coworker who was different from him, but who was perfect for him. One who completed him and the unit needed to fulfill God's directive to tend and populate the earth.

We have a tendency today to believe that in a healthy family, our children are a gift from God, when in reality, they are a trust. God has entrusted them to us for a short period of time. His purpose in creating the family was to build a place for children to grow, a place for them to learn to love God and to be people of integrity. It is not a place where adults just find pleasure and happiness, but where we find peace and fulfillment by accomplishing our true propose and meeting our responsibility as parents.

This plan God has for mankind is of course general and there are exceptions. Scripture says some are called to be single. Others become widows and widowers, and of course, though it is not God's desire, there are divorces that result in singleness. Single people can have healthy lives and families, but I believe it is like living with a handicap. They have to learn to compensate for that missing quality that a spouse would bring to their life. Maybe this is why God says He will be the defender of widows and the Father of orphans (Psalm 68:5).

God had a perfect plan for mankind and the family. It was a reflection of Heaven and Himself, but the plan was hindered by Satan. Only by looking to and following God's commands can we have a fruitful life in this physical world influenced by sin. Jesus came to show us how to have that life. He taught about the Kingdom of God, which is a way of living in this lifetime as well as a future hope (NIV Study Bible, Matthew 3:2 notes). Once, having been asked by the Pharisees when the Kingdom of God would come, Jesus replied, **"The Kingdom of God does not come with your careful observation, nor will people say, 'Here it is,' or, 'There it is,' because the Kingdom of God is with you" (Luke 17:20-21).**

The early Christian writers often spoke of the "way." The Kingdom of God is a way of living. There are two ways to live, one of life or one of death. The way that leads to peace, fulfillment and eternal life is a spiritual way of living. It can only be found by denying our self-centered, physical natures and embracing our spiritual natures that reflect the nature of God. The second way embraces the physical world and leads to darkness and death.

This godly way of living goes against our human natures, but it reflects our faith that our existence on this physical earth is a small, but important part of our total existence; immensely important because it determines how we will spend eternity.

# Notes

1.  Rick Warren, *The Purpose Driven Life*, (Grand Rapids, MI: Zondervan, 2002) p. 117.

2.  Taken from *Shade of His Hand* by Oswald Chambers, © 1936, 1995 by the Oswald Chambers Publications Assn., Ltd., p. 126. Used by permission of Discovery House Publishers, Grand Rapids, MI 49501. All rights reserved.

3.  Taken from *Biblical Psychology* by Oswald Chambers, © 1962 by the Oswald Chambers Publications Assn., Ltd., p. 25. Used by permission of Discovery House Publishers, Grand Rapids, MI 49501. All rights reserved.

4.  Chambers, *Shade of His Hand*, p. 125.

# Chapter 5

## *Take a Stand*

I believe women have always played an important part in God's kingdom. Down through history, the writers of scripture downplayed their role, but they were very important and they will continue to be used by God for mighty works. Very often in Old Testament scripture, the names of the mothers of kings are reported. I believe this is because the mother had a great influence on the kind of king they became. Women still have this influence and I believe they will play a large part in spreading the Gospel and returning our families back to God.

God used a woman to bring Jesus into this world. The seed of the woman defeats Satan. It was women who supported Jesus' ministry, who traveled with Him and provided for His needs. Jesus used women to teach some of the most important lessons of His ministry (living water, forgiveness, faith, giving, serving). When Jesus' male disciples fled, His women followers stayed loyal to Him, all the way to the cross. It was a woman He first appeared to after His resurrection and who spread this "good news" to the disciples.

Scripture recognizes the influence of women. They establish the spirit and heart of the home, or, through lack of wisdom and poor decisions, they can destroy a home.

> **The wise woman builds her house, but with her own hands the foolish one tears hers down. (Proverbs 14:1)**

The New American Standard version of the Bible is considered the most accurate translation by many theologians, although it is not the easiest to read.

> **The Lord gives the command; The women who proclaim the good tidings are a great host: "Kings of armies flee, they flee, And she who remains at home will divide the spoil. (Psalm 68:11-12 NAS)**

I believe this scripture indicates that the battle for our nation, and also our world, will be fought in our homes. The condition of our families reflects the condition of our nation, and it is obvious that our families are in trouble.

It is interesting that neither the King James nor the NIV translate this verse as *women* proclaiming God's word (good tiding). The NIV even says it is the men who will divide the spoils. This is an indication that women will play an important part in God's kingdom work. They just need to be encouraged and made aware of their value and influence. It is also a clear example of mistakes made in gender translation.

Ed Silvoso has written an amazing book called *Women, God's Secret Weapon*. Every Christian should read it. He explains God's plan for women and Satan's work to hinder it. Satan is working to keep women down because he knows it is women he needs to be afraid of since it is their seed that will defeat him.

# An Army of Women

Women need to discover this truth. The devil knows that God does not lie—what God promises always comes to pass. This is why Satan has spent centuries belittling women and weaving a web of lies into a formidable worldwide network of oppression to hold them down. He knows that when women find out who they really are, his evil kingdom will come to an abrupt end. He cannot afford to have women walking upright. He desperately needs to keep them down.

But Satan cannot do this forever. The Scriptures tell us that the day is fast approaching when God will lift women and release masses of them into ministry. Psalm 68:11 declares that at a strategic time God will give a command, and a company of women who proclaim the good news will defeat His enemies. An all-female army will bring this about and it will be a surprise victory. (1, Silvoso)

He goes on to explain that the devil's weapon to keep women down is conflict between men and women and that reconciliation between them is needed to thwart his plan.

God is leading others to bring this message out in the open. Jane Hansen of Aglow International, promotes reconciliation between men and women so that through their healthy relationships, God can be reflected on earth. Beth Moore is also exposing this strategy of Satan.

Satan desires to have women in a stronghold of exploitation, sexploitation, distortion, and desolation. He knows how effective and influential women can be, so he works through society to convince us we are so much less than we are. (2, Moore)

Satan strives to promote chaos and hate in both our families and the world. This is his goal, and Jesus came to counteract his activity. His weapon of choice is love and forgiveness. He said, love your neighbor, pray for your enemy, and forgive and you will be forgiven. He was promoting the power of good over evil. Good always wins out over evil. I believe this is the only answer to the hate and terrorism that is dominating our world today (2009). Hate cannot be eliminated by military power alone. It can only be overcome successfully by good, by love.

Women are the love-givers. No one can explain a mother's love, but it is the closest thing human that reflects God's agape love. It is an unconditional love that disapproves of bad behavior, but always continues to love; loving for who someone is, not what they do. Once you are born into the family of God, that love is always yours; even if you are a prodigal that has left the family. Even if you are living in a "pig pen" because of sinful behavior, you can always return to God and receive a child's welcome (Luke 15:15).

I believe this love is the catalyst that will heal our world. I also believe women are the initiators of this love. Whether it is in husbands, children or others, women can plant this seed in them and water it to produce healthy loving people. Sociologists have said that the future character and nature of a society rests in the hearts and minds of women.

The most receptive time of this influence is in early childhood, the time a mother needs the support and protection of her husband the most. This is why reconciliation between men and women is so important. Both play a major role in this process.

Our individual freedoms in the United States are wonderful, God-given rights, but we have let the pendulum swing too far one way. Were our founding fathers overreacting to oppressive monarchies when they promoted individual rights to such an extent; and was that why they stressed the need for strong moral values to balance these freedoms?

When important issues are debated among law-makers and the media, all that is promoted is the right of the individual. No one is discussing what is good for our nation. Is it good for our society that we have killed through abortion 40 million citizens in the last 40 years? What are the long-term societal affects of promoting homosexual relationships as normal? Divorce on demand hurts children, and what hurts children, hurts the future of our nation. It has been said the United States can only be destroyed from within. Is this a foreshadowing of what these "freedoms" could lead to?

It is time for women to take a stand for what is right and good, not just for themselves individually, but for women and children in general and society as a whole. We need to think about how our actions affect our own family, but we also need to be aware that, as a group, our actions influence society for good or for bad. Girls from the cradle through the innocent childhood years and into young adulthood are watching us. They are learning how to be, not only wives and mothers, but hopefully women of integrity who know their importance and influence in the world. They are learning how to relate to men, what is acceptable, and what is not. Just as the Holy Spirit is our counselor and teacher, Proverbs promotes mothers as teachers and it is important for them to instill these basic truths in their children.

We need to teach girls the importance they play in shaping our society; yes, in the workforce, but more importantly, in our families. When we start to value, not only our daughters, but also all women for their hearts, minds and character, we will empower them to fill their God-given position. This is a position of influence, equality, and partnership with men.

Mothers and fathers need to raise their sons to respect

and protect girls and women. It needs to be instilled in them at an early age that they are the protectors of future families and societies.

It is time for men to take a stand and do, not the easiest thing, or the most pleasurable, but what is right and healthy for families and society. To not only stay in marriages, but to provide the leadership required to produce healthy children; daughters who know their value and potential and sons who will one day be strong husbands, fathers and leaders. When in the position to do so, they need to prevent the exploitation and oppression of women, whether in the home, the workplace or society.

As said before, men are the leaders of their families and God holds them responsible for the health of their families.

> **"I will not punish your daughters when they turn to prostitution, nor your daughter-in-laws when they commit adultery, because the men themselves consort with harlots and sacrifice with shrine prostitutes—a people without understanding will come to ruin!" (Hosea 4:14)**

It is time for our politicians and other influential people in government to take a stand for a healthy society. This means promoting legislation and policies that are good for our families and our nation and not to line their pockets or increase their power and influence.

This is such an exciting time for women around the world. Muslim women in the Middle East are on the verge of a changed life, and all women should be supportive and encouraging of this process. I do not know how they will view the Holy Spirit being feminine, but if they are true followers of the God of Abraham and Muhammad, it will change their view of Jehovah God and greatly influence their faith and lives.

It is obvious from the Koran that Muhammad was a true believer in Jehovah God, Allah, the God of Abraham and Moses; the God who authored the Old Testament scripture that promotes this equal partnership between men and women. Muhammad was told to "read," and he devoted himself to learning the Old Testament. He received the truth of the Holy Spirit and Her work of spreading the knowledge of Jehovah God among mankind, but he must have concluded She was just a part of the one God. He acknowledged Jesus as a great prophet, but he never came to accept Him as God because Scripture clearly taught against polytheism, and he could not accept the idea of the Trinity.

Today, Muslims seem to ignore the Old Testament and the fact that it was Muhammad's Bible (The Book). The Koran will always be important to Muslims, but it is time for them to also accept Scripture as part of the true teachings of God. They not only oppress women, but they teach hatred and violence toward Christians and Jews. Muhammad never promoted violence toward followers of his own God, the God of Abraham and Moses. If Muhammad were here today, he would also say, "read," not just the Koran, but also the Old Testament. Many of the Islamic faith are promoting teachings of men who have other motivations than teaching the truth of God.

Because of male dominance, half of Muslim intelligence, talent and wisdom has been suppressed for thousands of years. This has resulted in an unbalanced society where violence and revenge is promoted by an influential portion of the population. If women are allowed to take their rightful place alongside men, we may see an amazing establishment of a new, progressive society in that area. With the advent of world wide communications and information, the time is ripe for women of the world to rise to their rightful position of influence.

I do hope that when eastern women look to the west to see what women have accomplished in the area of equal rights, they will see and learn from the mistakes we made. I encourage the women of that area to embrace the good that has come from our movement, and try to avoid the excesses western society has accepted. They should not discard the good that is embodied in their traditions.

Most important, they need to realize they are the key to peace and prosperity in their nations. If they make a stand for what is right and good for their families and promote love and respect for one another, they could start a movement that may take a couple of generations, but that could change the world.

Another area of the world where I see this phenomenon causing a grave problem is China. Because of the lack of respect and appreciation for the role women play in their society, sons have been preferred over daughters. The one-child policy has lead to aborting girls, abandoning them to die and giving them away to countries around the world. Not only is their nation becoming unbalanced because of a lack of feminine influence, but they are actually raising a generation of young men with a shortage of women to marry and have families with.

Here in America, we have a choice. We can continue to participate in behavior that leads to the deterioration of our families and the decline of our nation, or we can recognize and promote a way of living that is healthy for us individually and also as a people. America has great influence in the world. I like to think it is primarily for good. By setting an example for the young women of the world, we can change our world for the better.

# Notes

1.  Ed Silvoso, *Women, God's Secret Weapon*, (Ventura, CA: Regal Books, 2001) p. 17.
2.  Beth Moore, *Breaking Free* (Bible Study), (Nashville, TN: Lifeway Press, 1999) p. 119.

# *Conclusion*

There are those who believe man has created God *in his own image* to fill his psychological needs and to use as a crutch, as some say. This is a theory that can be substantiated in other religions, especially New Ageism. They have taken the parts of God they like and made a religion pleasing to man. They offer a god who allows self-determination and self-gratification, promoting only the feel-good, loving side of God. But Jehovah God created all things and made the rules for heaven, earth and mankind. It is this God who requires the *unnatural* from man, and because of our human nature, it is not easy to follow Him. Our human nature promotes the self-centered, selfish desires of the flesh, a desire to be autonomous. God calls us to be submissive to His laws, to deny self and put others and their welfare before our own. They call us to put God and spiritual things before human and earthly things. Scripture introduces us to this one true God.

This truth about the Holy Spirit is just one example of our God being the one true God, Jehovah (YHWH), I am who I am. He is not who men want Him to be, but He is who He is. Man's rejection of the femininity of the Holy Spirit did not change God. The truth and fact is still there, and with study and the inspiration of the Holy Spirit, God's truth will always come out in His time.

Segments of our society try to convince us that truth is relative. There are psychological differences among people that make them respond differently, but the laws of nature, and the laws of God, do not change.

God has clearly given mankind free will to either choose Him or the natural, fallen world; life or death. Life is an existence focused on God and spiritual things. Death is a self-centered life focusing on the world and physical gratification. He gave Adam and Eve the choice of life and death. Life was obedience to Him, which resulted in fellowship with Him and living in paradise. By disobeying Him (eating of the tree of the knowledge of good and evil), they found death, not an immediate physical death, but spiritual death. They were separated from God and lost God's blessing. This resulted in having to leave the Garden of Eden and having to make their way in a fallen world.

God used Abraham and then Moses to bring the Israelites back into fellowship with Him. He introduced the blood sacrifice as the means of forgiveness of sins that opens the way to communion with Him: first the atonement sacrifice of the Old Testament (or covenant), second Jesus Christ as the last, perfect, blood sacrifice for all mankind of the New Testament (or covenant). Christianity teaches we must receive Jesus Christ as our Lord and Savior to access this personal relationship with God. There are many sincere believers in Jehovah God today (Jews and Muslims included) who seek His face and live to please Him, but they do not accept Jesus as their Savior or the Son of God. I do not know how God relates to these followers, but I do know those who receive Jesus as their Savior and Son of God are called children of God and are promised the gift of the Holy Spirit.

The greatest lesson of both the Old and New Testaments is God's call for his people to obey Him and His commands. Many Christians believe the Old Testament is obsolete. Even though Jesus came to reconcile us to God and change the way we approach God, we should not ignore the Old Testament. It is filled with much insight as to who God is and how to live a life pleasing to Him. God did not create man to be a robot, to love Him automatically. If this were the case, the relationship would have no value. God gave man free will to either choose Him and to love Him or not. When the Israelites followed God, they had peace and prosperity. When they turned their backs on Him, they temporarily enjoyed earthly and fleshly pleasures, but it always lead to "death" and destruction.

We are part of this pattern today. Years ago, our society turned away from God and His plan and turned toward earthly and physical pleasures. We have chosen a physical path over a spiritual one. We are now reaping the results of that choice. All we have to do is look at the state of our children and families to see this. The only way back is to return to God and His plan.

God to this day puts before us a choice. Both the Old and New Testaments put the ball in our court. Whether a person chooses to live under the law of the Old Testament (servant-hood), or the grace Jesus offers us (sonship), he needs to seek the truth of God and be willing to submit his life to that truth. Choose God and His ways and He is faithful to His promises. He may not give us an *easy* life, but with time, He will lead us into a life that is real and full of purpose, a life that is empowered by his glorious presence.

Jehovah God says,

> **...I have set before you life and death, blessings and curses. Now choose life so that you and your children may live and that you may love the Lord your God, listen to his voice, and hold fast to him... (Deuteronomy 30:19-20)**

Jesus says,

> **...I came that they might have life, and might have it abundantly. (John 10:10, NAS)**

What will you choose?

# *Epilogue*

As I mentioned in the introduction, I want this book to initiate a dialogue on this subject. If you have information you think is pertinent, please send it to me. Every effort was made to be completely accurate, but if you see a mistake, please bring that to my attention also. My goal was to present the evidence in a short, easy to read format, but if there is enough new information, it could lead to a revision.

Please send comments to holy-spirit@hotmail.com.

Blessings,
Patricia Taylor

Printed in Great Britain
by Amazon